You Need to Hear This

365 DAYS OF SILLY, HONEST
ADVICE YOU NEED RIGHT NOW

CHRONICLE BOOKS
SAN FRANCISCO

Library of Congress Cataloging-in-Publication
Data available.
ISBN 978-1-7972-0769-8

Manufactured in China.

Design by Rachel Harrell.
Typesetting by Kelly Abeln.
Text by Dena Rayess.

10 9 8 7 6 5 4 3 2

Chronicle books and gifts are available at special quantity
discounts to corporations, professional associations, literacy
programs, and other organizations. For details and discount
information, please contact our premiums department at
corporatesales@chroniclebooks.com or at 1-800-759-0190.

Chronicle Books LLC
680 Second Street
San Francisco, California 94107
www.chroniclebooks.com

HEY THERE,

We all need a little guidance now and then. Maybe it's a pep talk from your bestie, a kind word from someone you respect, or a bit of too-real advice from a parent. Getting some direction can make all the difference in your day, year, or life. But sometimes, it's hard to find the right words.

This little book has 365 pieces of advice, something for every life moment. Think of it like an oracle deck, a Magic 8 Ball, or an irreverent tarot reading.

Not sure what to do? *Say yes to more cheese.*

Feeling burned out? *You are worth more than your productivity.*

Need some uplifting words? *Good news, you're perfect.*

Crack this book open at random or flip through the colorful pages until you find the one that feels right. Keep the words with you throughout the day. Come back to them for answers, a moment of clarity, or a quick chuckle.

No matter what, *You Need to Hear This.*

YOU HAVE FOOD AT HOME

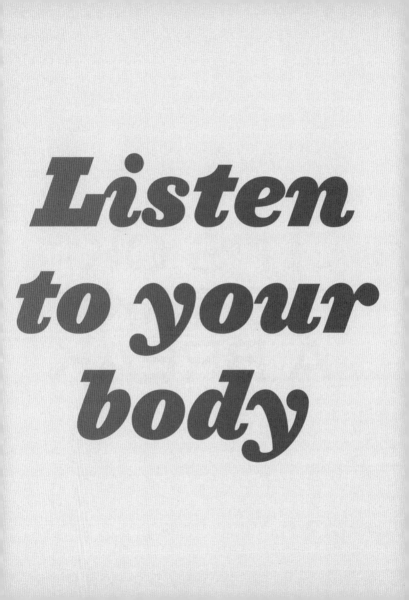

IT'S OK TO TAKE A BREAK

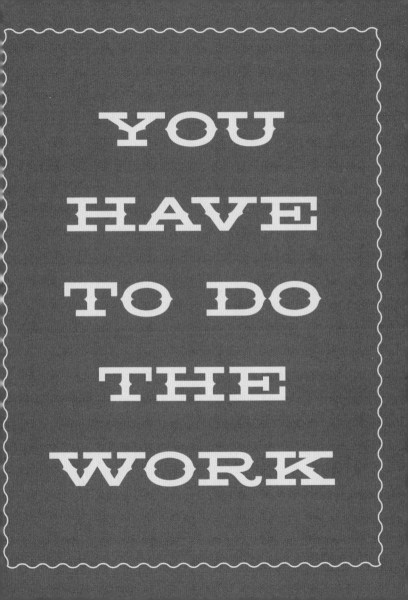

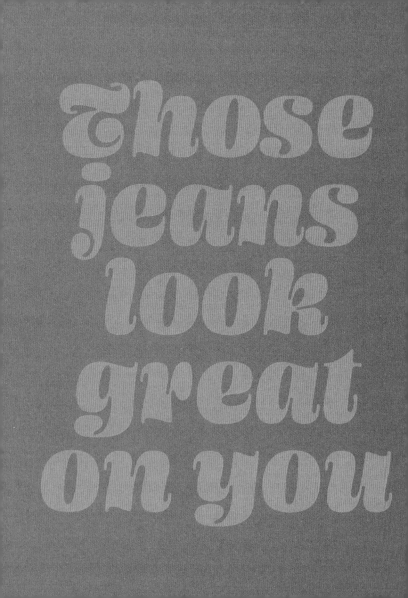

Doing nothing is something

You're actually doing just fine

STOP WORKING AFTER 6 P.M.

"Family-size"
can be
for a family
of one

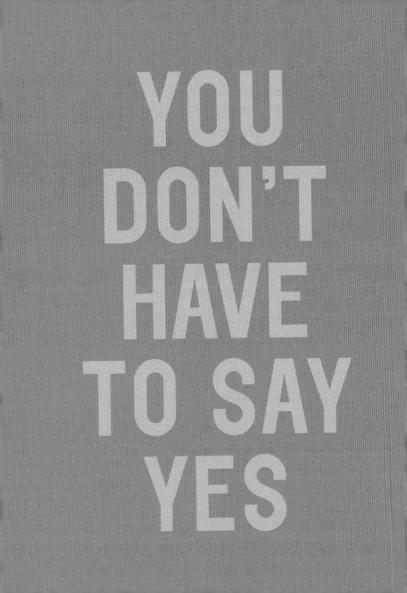

Go
slow

TAKE
A NAP

Stretchy pants are technically pants

Take ten
deep breaths

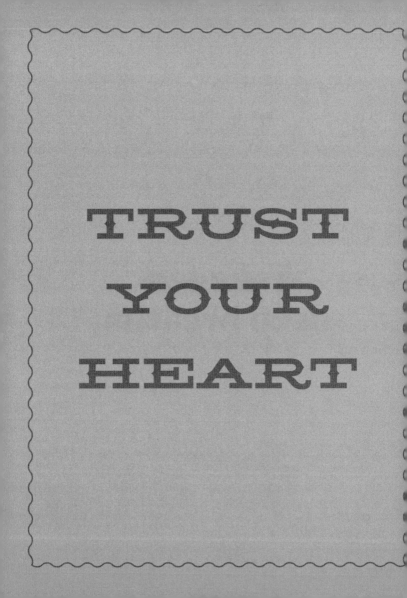

call your bff

DRY SHAMPOO IS NOT A SHOWER

Thank yourself

WRITE
IT
DOWN

SLEEP

ON IT

Make a list

GIVE YOURSELF CREDIT

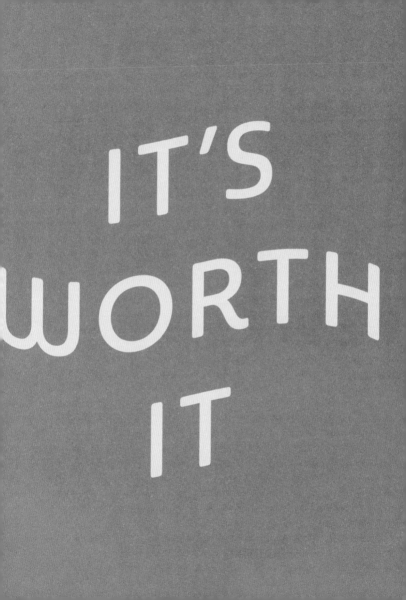

DRINK
SOME
WATER

EAT DESSERT FIRST

You are
more than
enough

TAKE A SCREEN BREAK

IT'S GOING TO BE FINE

IS IT REALLY WORTH IT?

Sweatpants
count as
real pants

LET GO OF ONE THING TODAY

Redirect
yourself

HIT THE SNOOZE BUTTON

Take time to daydream

What could
you do
differently?

HAVE A
COOKIE

stop and

smell the

flowers

make
some art

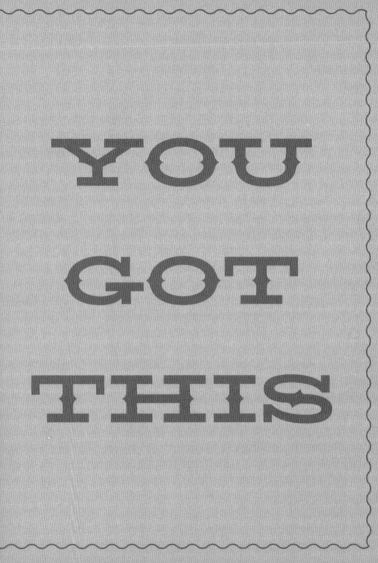
YOU GOT THIS

There are endless possibilities

Check
in with
yourself

ASK
AGAIN

PUSH YOUR
BOUNDARIES

what's
the worst
that could
happen?

VISUALIZE
IT

TODAY IS

BRAND NEW

QUESTION
THE
ANSWER

Everything must end

MOVE WITH PURPOSE

TEA

BOSS

DANCE IT OUT

LOVE

WINS

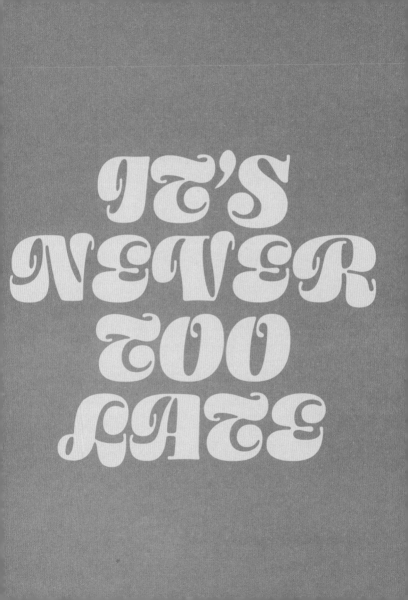

YOU know
what's best
for you

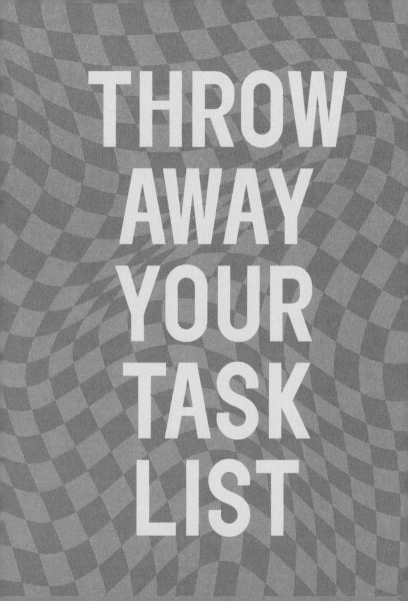

Make time for yourself

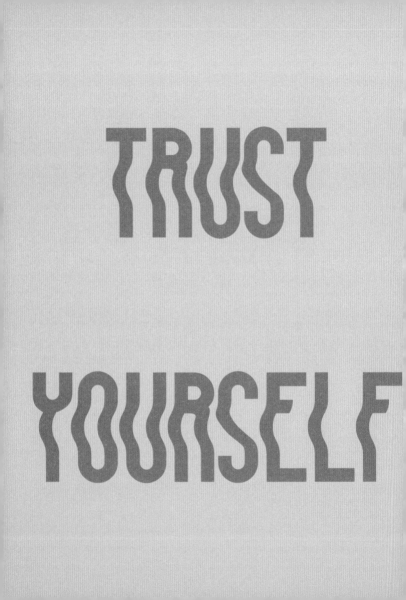

YOU
ARE
WORTHY

You're supercool

TAKE A
SNACK BREAK

DON'T AVOID REALITY

THERE'S
NO RUSH

FIND A QUIET PLACE

Eat something

:)

Give yourself
permission

You're the best

BE
FEARLESS

Pay attention
to the details

YOU'RE WORTH MORE

LOOK
FOR
CLUES

take
the scenic
route

celebrate
anything
and
everything

Embrace change

SAY
"SORRY"
LESS

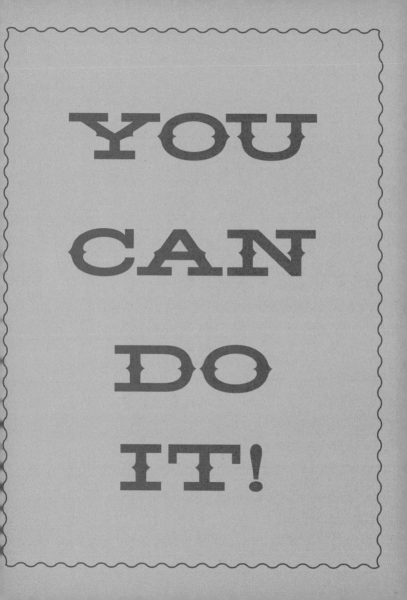

DON'T LET THEM GET YOU DOWN

SAY WHAT YOU REALLY MEAN

Eat more veggies

KEEP IN
TOUCH

ENJOY IT WHILE IT LASTS

Don't

forget to

breathe

Set boundaries

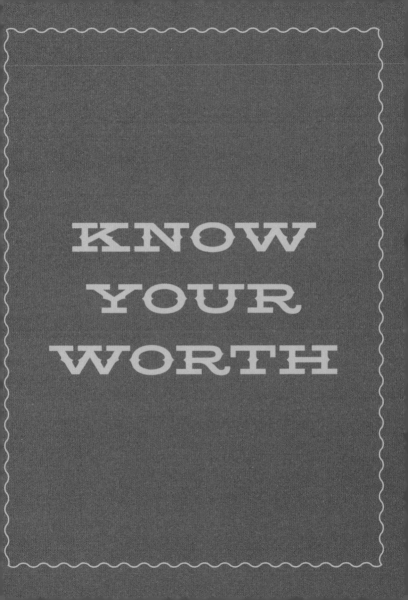

KNOW

YOUR

WORTH

LEAN
INTO IT

Don't forget
to have fun

TALK TO SOMEONE

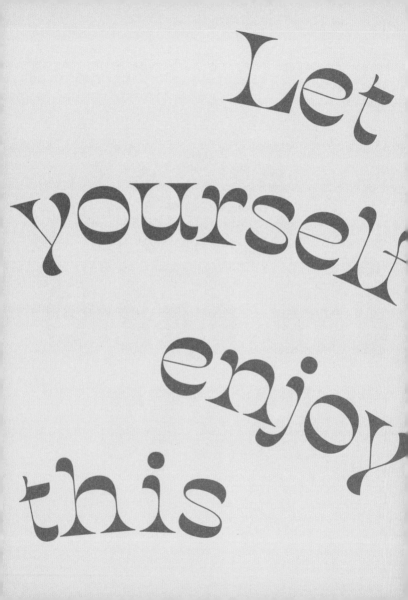

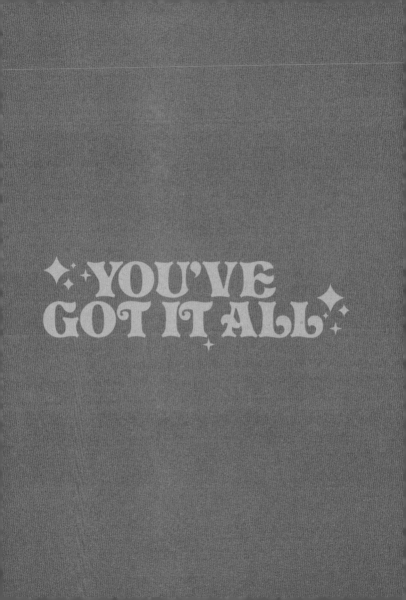

BE
PREPARED

Do something different

TAKE
A LONG
BATH

You are more than this moment

PICK YOUR BATTLES

Set an intention

EMBRACE THE PRESENT

GET
PHYSICAL

Investigate that feeling

OPEN YOUR HEART

EXPRESS
YOURSELF

Help
yourself
first

MAKE SPACE FOR YOURSELF

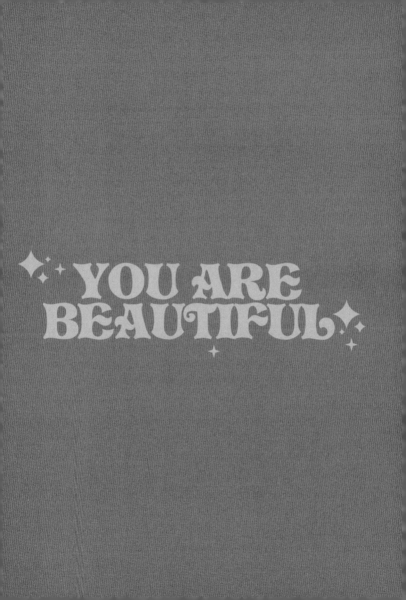

ADVOCATE FOR YOURSELF

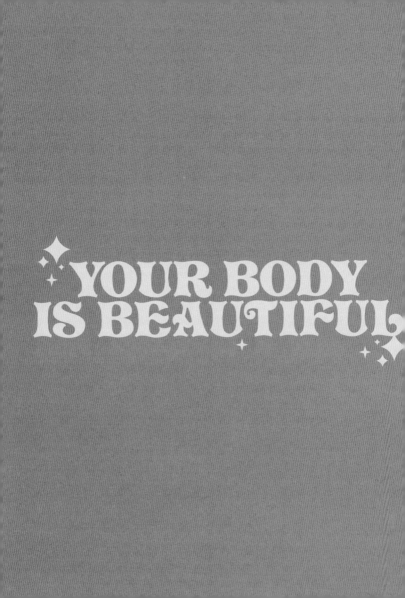

There is nothing in your way

What does your heart tell you?

IT'S OK TO BE OPEN

Listen to them

YOU
KNOW
THE
WAY

LOVE
YOURSELF
FIRST

SHOW
UP

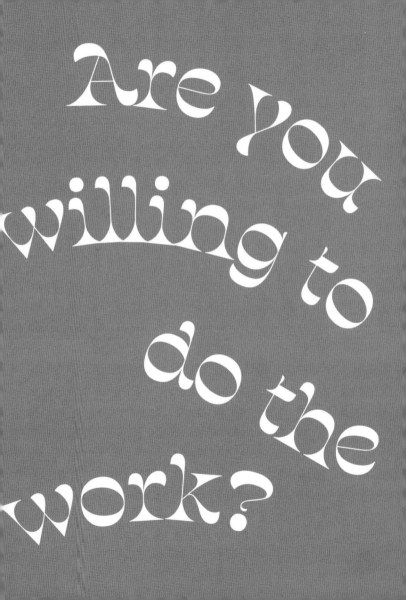

CELEBRATE YOUR ABILITIES

Be
vulnerable

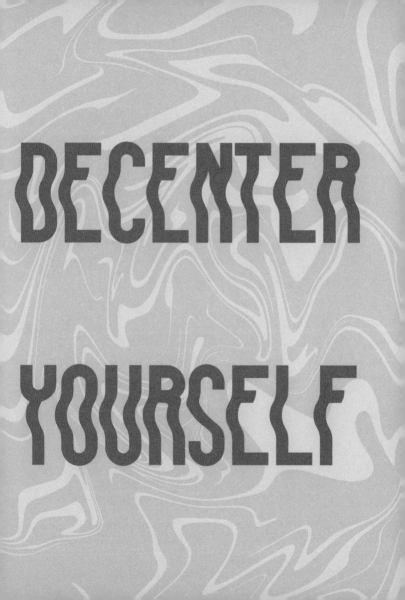

CHECK IN ON
YOUR FRIENDS

The call is
coming from
inside the house

SOMETIMES IT'S BETTER NOT TO KNOW

THANK YOUR

MISTAKES

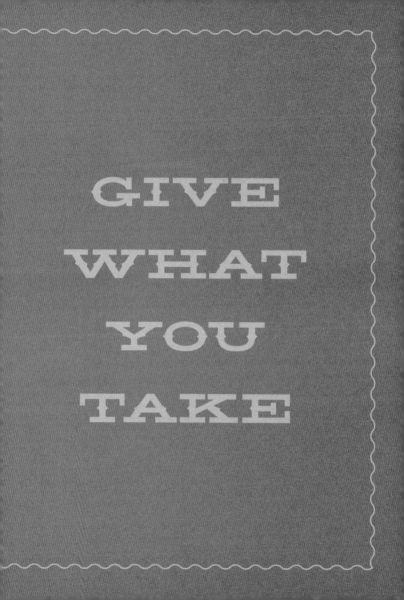

GIVE
WHAT
YOU
TAKE

YOU ARE
WORTH MORE
THAN YOUR
PRODUCTIVITY

GIVE YOURSELF A PEP TALK

Love is never a waste

FOCUS
ON WHAT
YOU CAN
CONTROL

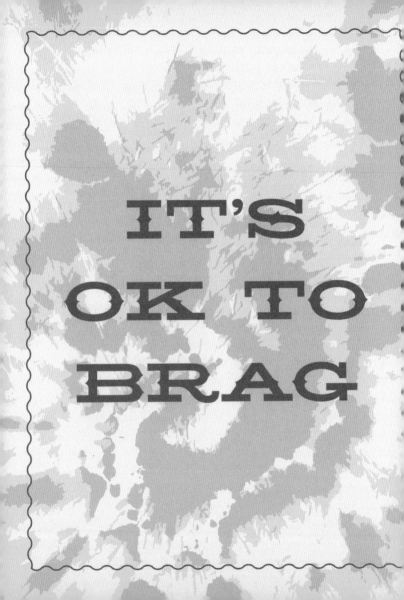

IT'S OK TO BRAG

BE KIND TO YOUR PAST SELF

THINGS WILL WORK OUT

THINGS
WILL
CHANGE
WITH
TIME

YOU ARE
ALLOWED
TO GROW

Don't compare your journey to the journey of others

you don't
need to be happy
all the time
:(

WHAT DO YOU NEED?

It's always the right time for pizza

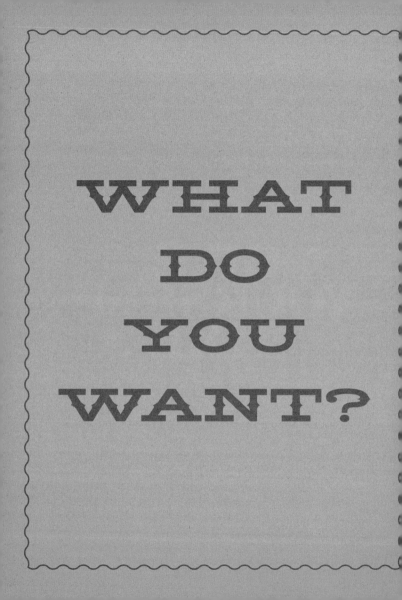

WHAT DO YOU WANT?

NO
ADULTING
TODAY

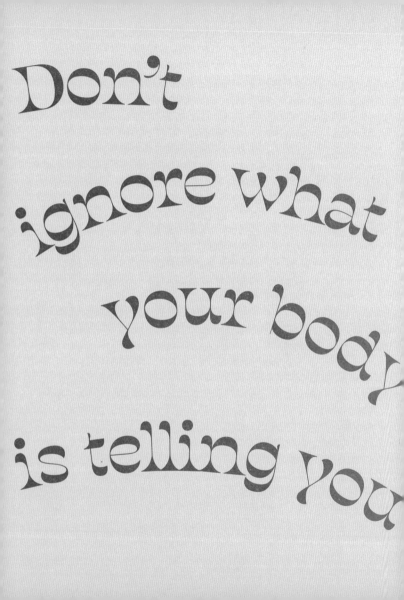

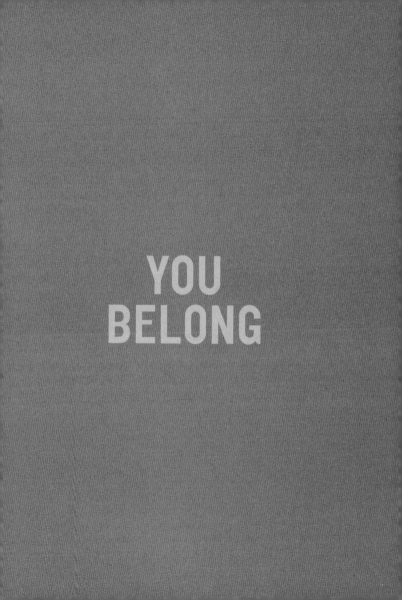

GROWTH
ISN'T LINEAR

WHERE ARE YOU GOING?

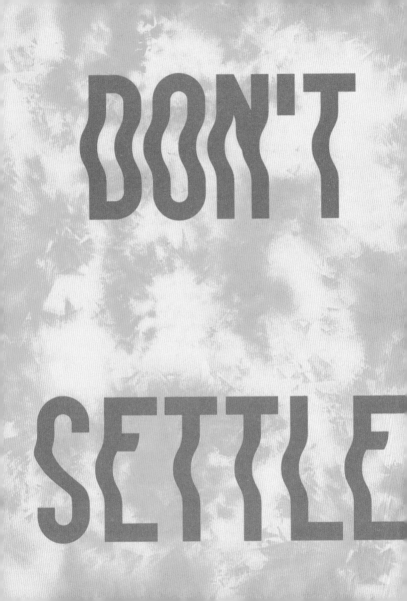

forget
about
your
phone

HANDLE YOUR BUSINESS

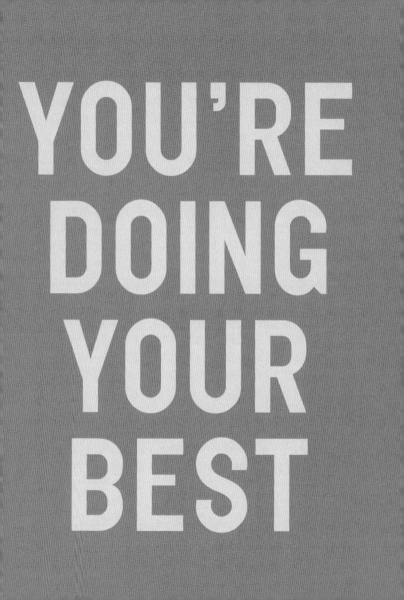

THERE IS NO SUCH THING AS TOO MANY HUGS

ASK "WHY" MORE

Embrace the chaos

Give more encouragement and less advice

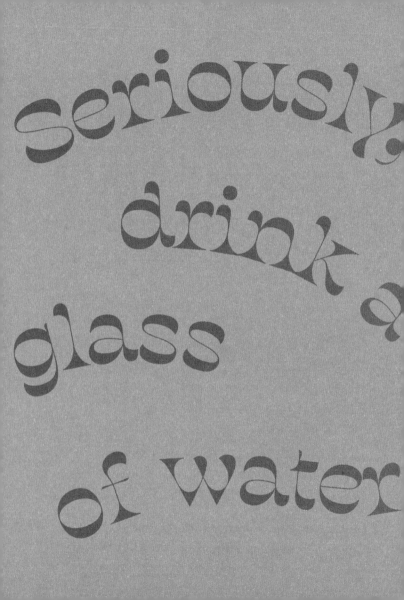

Joy is a
radical act

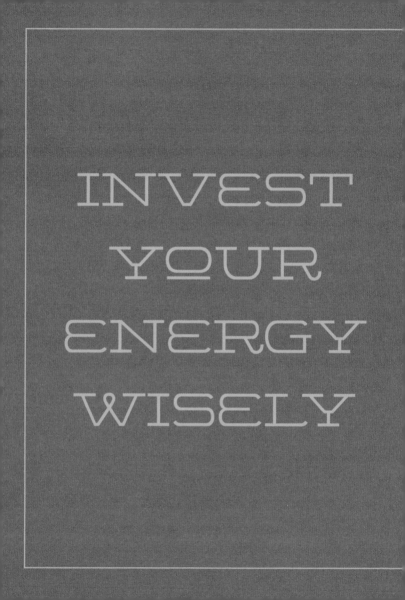

IT'S OK
TO OUTGROW
THINGS

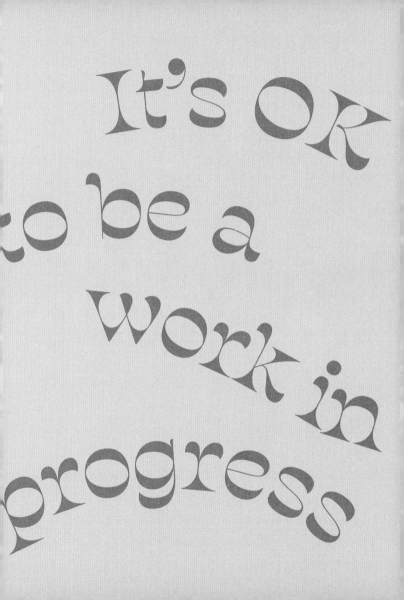

SHIFT YOUR PERSPECTIVE

KEEP
IT
UP

F*ck
it

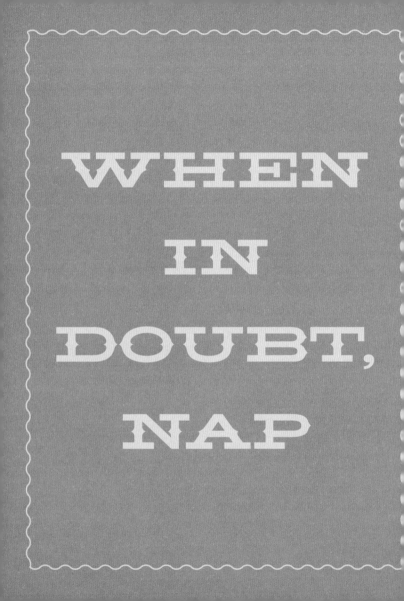

Question
the reason

PRIORITIZE YOUR PASSIONS

SELF-CARE IS NOT SELFISH

Focus on
progress, not
perfection

PRESS

FAUZE

Pet all
the dogs

SHOW YOU CARE

Don't forget why
you're doing it

TELL YOUR FRIENDS YOU LOVE THEM

You deserve better

EMBRACE YOUR POWER

TRUST YOUR

INTUITION

Don't compare yourself to people on the internet

It doesn't have
to make sense

KNOW YOUR RIGHTS

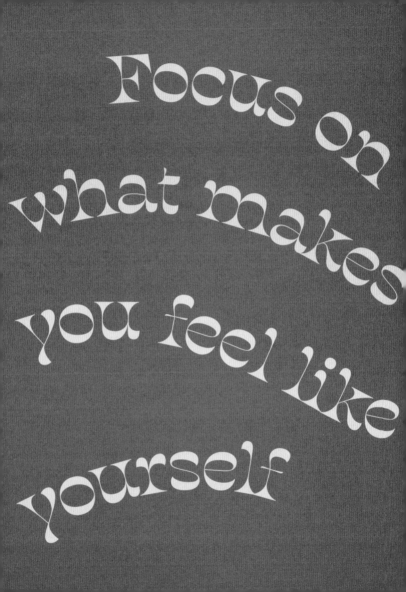

DON'T MAKE PERMANENT DECISIONS BASED ON TEMPORARY EMOTIONS

SH*T
HAPPENS

THE
SUN
WILL
ALWAYS
RISE

You have to
take care of
yourself first

DELETE THEIR NUMBER

Nothing
lasts forever

QUICK
FIXES
DON'T
LAST
LONG

Your direction
is more important
than your speed

SURVIVING
IS ENOUGH

Demand
respect

CRY
WHEN
YOU
WANNA

YOU'RE GOING TO MAKE IT

Celebrate

your

successes

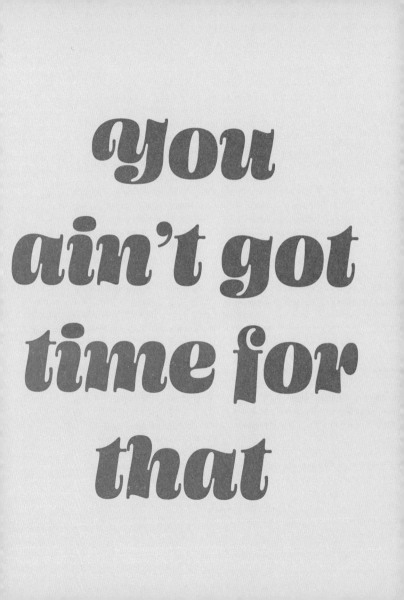

Sometimes the grass looks greener because it's fake

BE KIND TO YOUR MIND

STOP PLAYING CATCH-UP

If it's not 100% "yes," it's a no

STOP WATERING DEAD PLANTS

Worries can be valid

Savor the moment

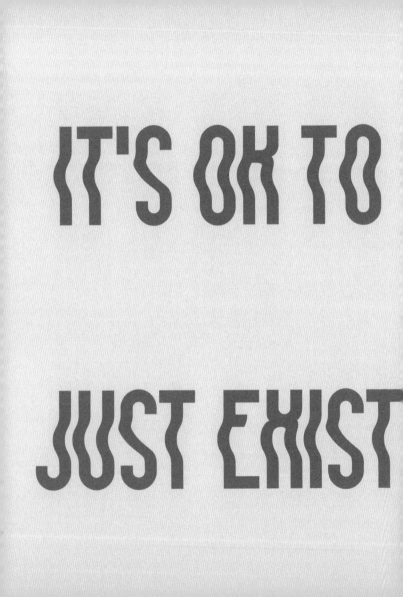

DITCH YOUR TO-DO LIST

Get out of
your own way

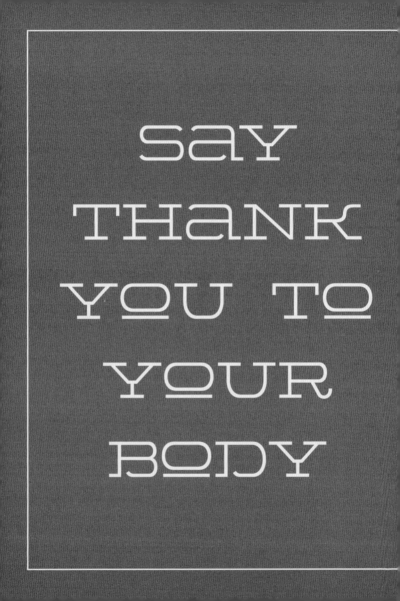

REMEMBER WHO YOU ARE

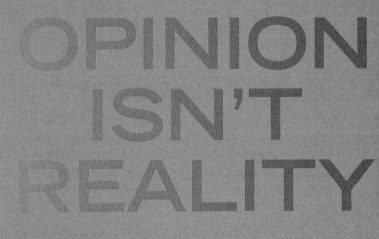

OPINION
ISN'T
REALITY

CRY OVER
SPILLED MILK

DON'T BE AFRAID TO START OVER

GIVE CREDIT WHERE CREDIT IS DUE

Do what
you can
with the
energy
you have

TAKE WHAT YOU NEED

your offline life matters more

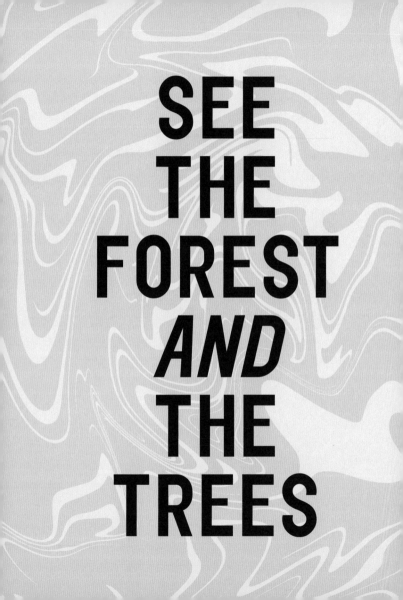

You can be
compassionate
and strong

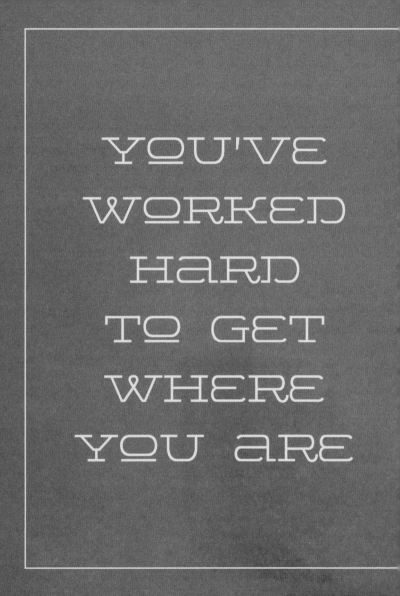

If you see
something,
say something

LOVE LEADS TO HEALING

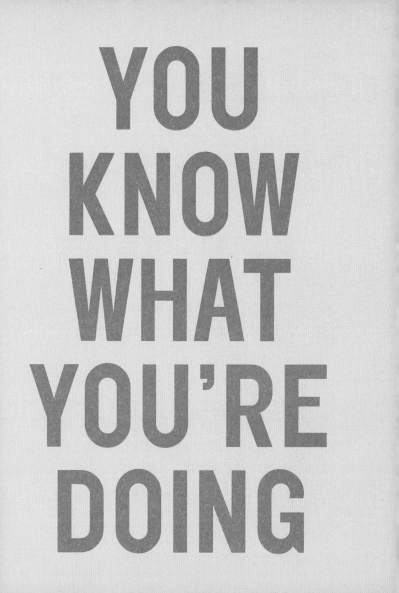

Good news,
you're perfect

YOU'RE
NOT
ALONE

You'll never feel 100% ready, and that's OK

MAKE TIME TO CREATE

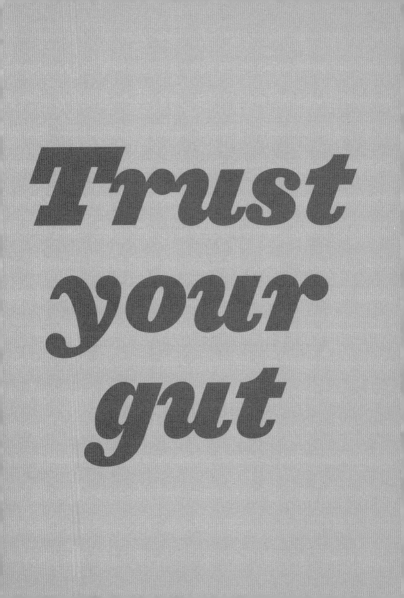

BUY YOURSELF FLOWERS

COMPLIMENTS
ARE FREE

Push through self-doubt

CONSIDER
EVERY
OUTCOME

A dream job
is still a job

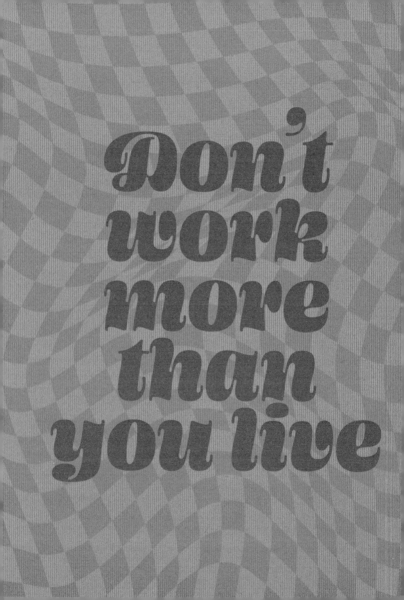

ACKNOWLEDGE THE GOOD

Relaxation
is a hobby

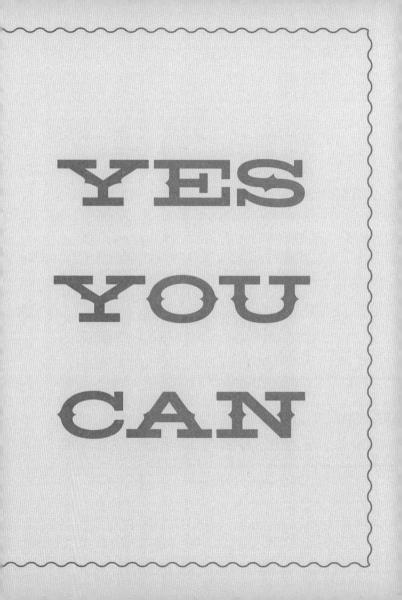

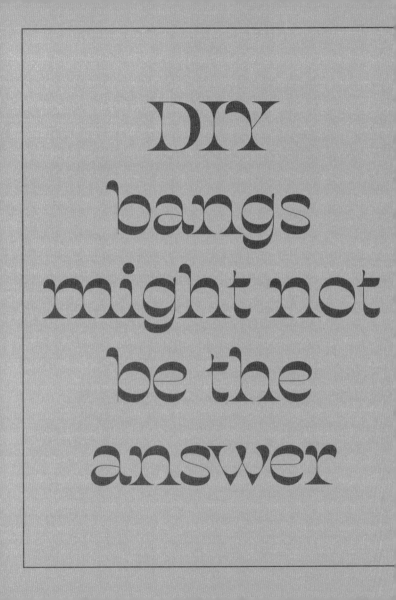

Don't worry, baby,
everything will
turn out alright

START
NEW

IT'S
OK TO
OUTGROW
PEOPLE

SNACK TIME CAN BE ANY TIME

RIDE THE WAVE

Add "me time" to your to-do list

HAVE
PRIDE

BUY SOME STRETCHY PANTS

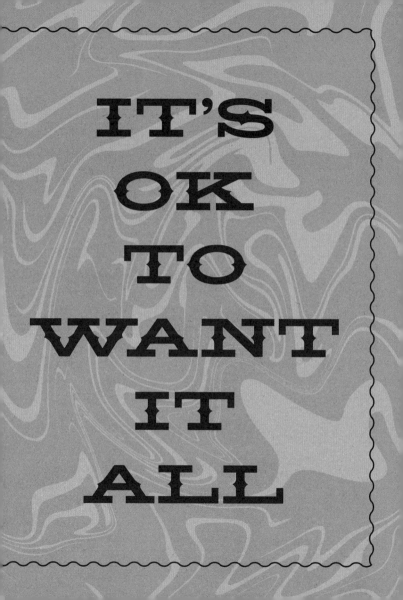

STOP CHECKING THE NEWS

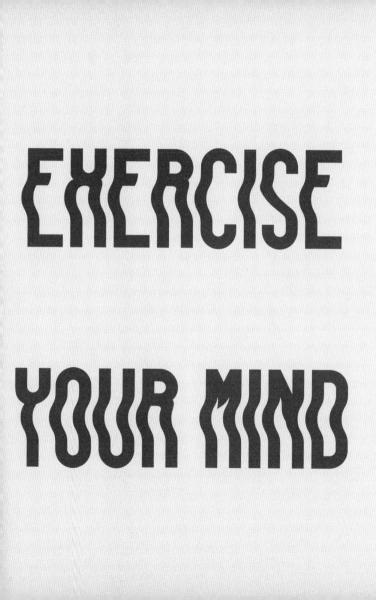

IT'S NEVER TOO LATE TO DREAM

GO AHEAD, BUY TWO

See what happens if you don't give up

DIY BANGS *MAY* BE THE ANSWER

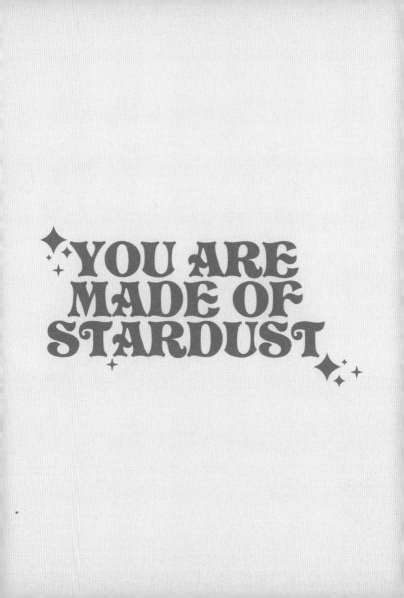

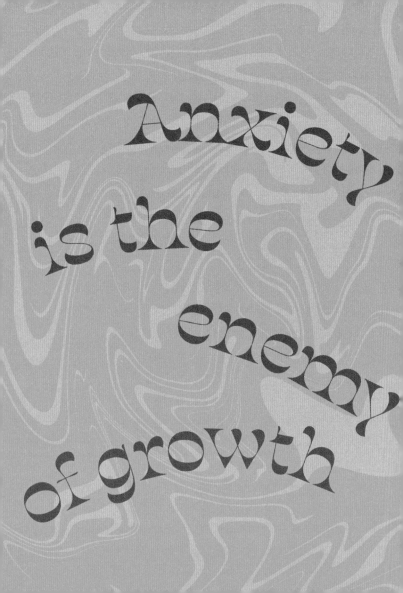

MAKE IT HAPPEN

Shock
everyone

YOU
MATTER

Give
someone a
compliment
today